Nurse Dotty

Molly Watts

There was once an owl called Dotty,
A nurse with a uniform all spotty.

She works in the hospital up the hill,
Looking after all the children who are ill.

Each morning nurse Dotty puts on her
uniform and hat,
Then she gets her bag that is sitting by the
mat.

She packs her books and plenty of food for the day,
Then goes out the door and is on her way.

Nurse Dotty arrives before she has to start,
First she looks for her name on the hospital
chart.

It tells nurse Dotty who she will be looking after and where,
So once she knows she can go and find them there.

Before nurse Dotty can meet her patient
and say hello,
There are some things about them that she
must first know.

So she asks the nurse that has been looking after them overnight,
And she tells nurse Dotty everything like their weight and their height.

Nurse Dotty takes some notes then she is ready to start;
She goes to her patient and listens to their heart.

On their chest and tummy her stethoscope also goes,
As she checks the patient over from their head to their toes.

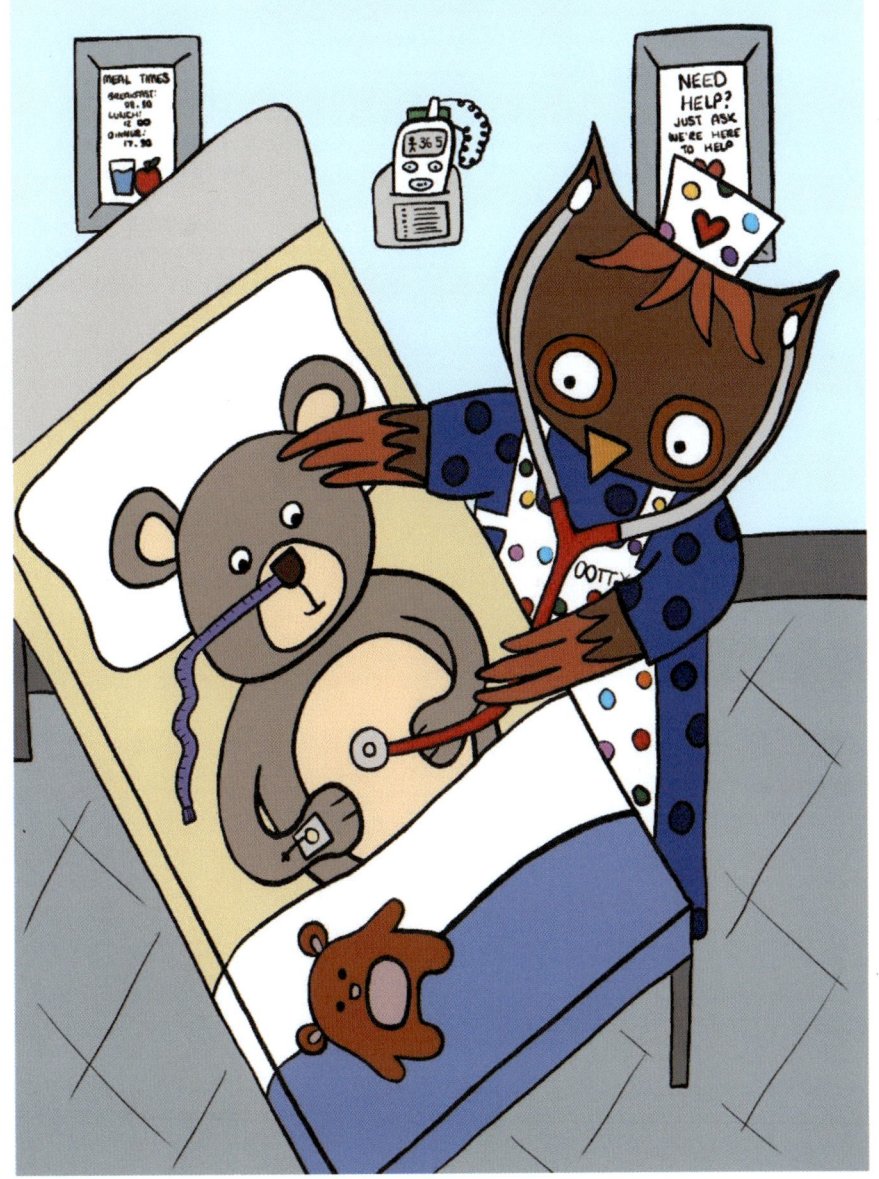

Now that she knows they are doing okay, Nurse Dotty makes a plan for the rest of the day.

She writes a list of when all the medicine is due,
Plus all of the other jobs that she needs to do.

Nurse Dotty regularly checks her patient to
see how they have been,
She takes their numbers then their chart
she fills in.

To do this she puts a probe on their finger
with a funny red dot,
The she uses the thermometer to see if
they are hot.

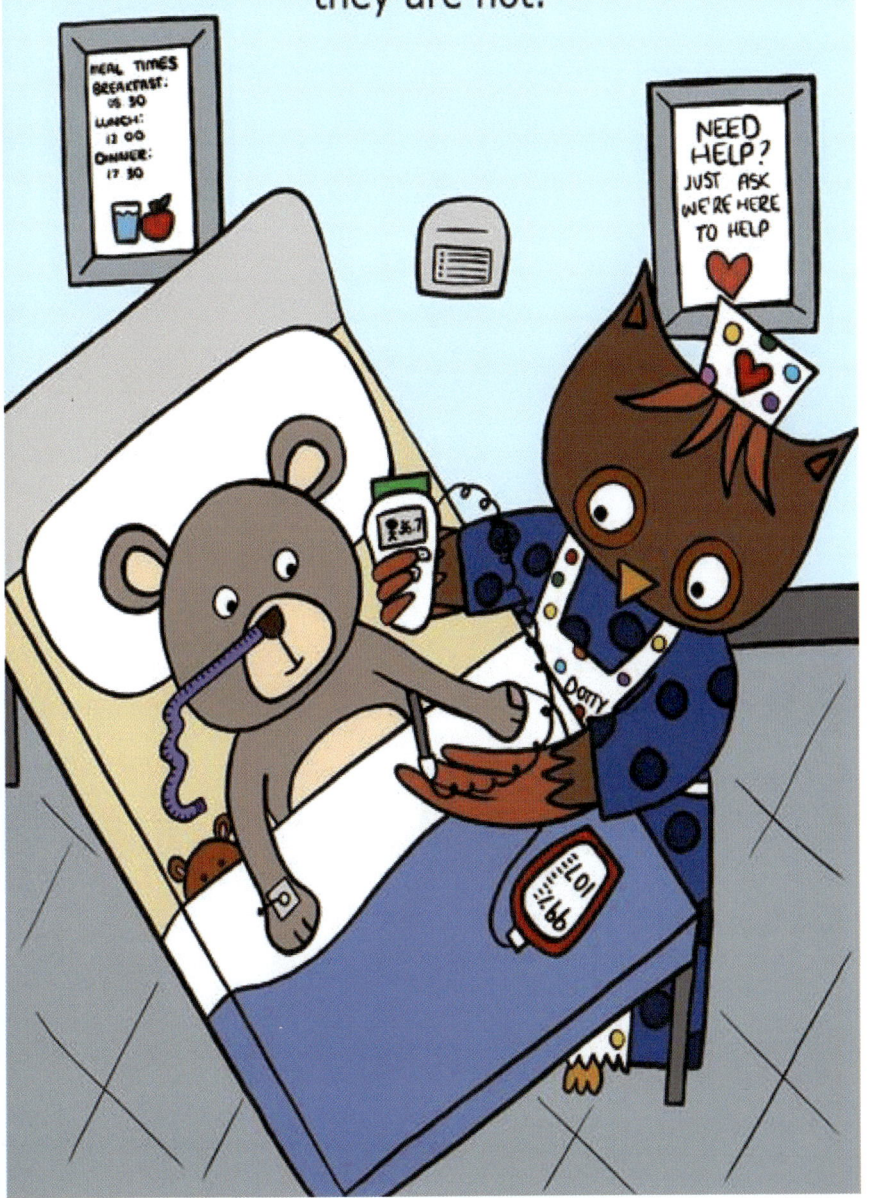

The patient has lines in their hand and a tube in their nose too,
Nurse Dotty uses these to give medicine and food through.

She gets the medicine ready by giving their chart a read,
It helps her to make sure they get exactly what they need.

Then nurse Dotty makes sure they are comfy in their bed or a chair,
Checking they have everything they want whilst she is there.

She gives them the button they can press
to give her a call,
Telling them to use it if they need anything
at all.

There is lots of others nurse Dotty has to go talk to,
With all sorts of uniforms and different things that they do.

From doctors to physios they all work together,
Using all their different skills to help make the patient better.

Nurse Dotty also makes sure there is time
to draw and play,
So that her patient doesn't get bored whilst
in hospital they stay.

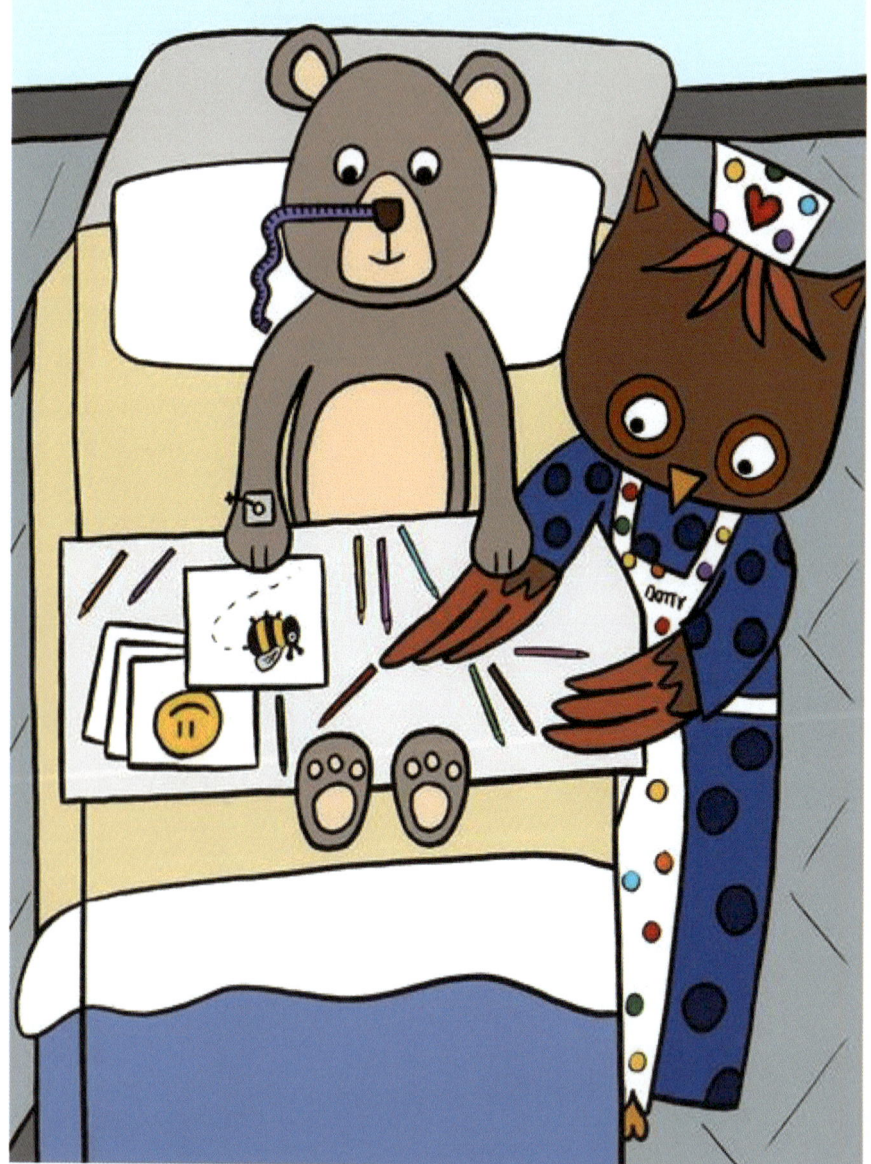

They make puppets out of gloves and hats for their head,
So much fun can be had from a hospital bed.

Having crossed jobs off her list as they are done,
At the end of the day nurse Dotty now has none.

Now all that is left are her notes so she finds a seat,
Then writes all about her patient; from medicine to heart beat.

When the busy day finally comes to an end, Nurse Dotty hands the patient back over to her friend.

Then she gets her things and heads out of the door,
Home to bed ready to come back tomorrow for more

About Nurse Dotty Books

Nurse Dotty books aim to alleviate anxiety around being admitted to hospital for children and their families through giving truthful information in a reassuring and friendly manner.

They are packed with pictures and references to equipment and procedures presented through a rhyming story with cartoon illustrations. This helps to, in a child friendly manner, introduce and explain some of the experiences they will have during theirs or a family members hospital admission.

To find out more

visit nurse Dotty online at:
www.nursedottybooks.com

find nurse Dotty on Facebook or Instagram at:
NurseDottyBooks

find nurse Dotty on Twitter at:
BooksDotty

Meet the author

My name is Molly Watts.

I am a registered children's nurse who has worked for a number of years in a paediatric intensive care unit.

Over those years I have written and illustrated a number of stories and poems for my little patients and it was through writing those stories that I was inspired to create nurse Dotty.

Printed in Germany
by Amazon Distribution
GmbH, Leipzig

17968286R00018